~Introducing Fiqh
Vol.9

Introducing the *Fiqh* of Clothing and Dress
(فقه اللباس)

Written and compiled by
SAFARUK Z. CHOWDHURY

AD-DUHA
LONDON 2008

©Ad-Duha, London 2010

First edition 2008

Updated Edition 2010

An educational publication from Ad-Duha London
Third Floor, 42 Fieldgate Street
London E1 1ES
E: info@duha.org.uk
W: www.duha.org.uk
T: 07891 421 925

Contents Page

Section:	Page
Table of Abbreviations	5
Table of Symbols	5
§1. Introduction	6-8
§2. Some Preliminary *Fiqh* Rules	9-11
§3. Clothing Guidelines from Imam Ibn 'Abidin's *Radd al-Muhtar*.	12-15
§4. The Categories of Clothing	16-20
§5. Imam al-Quduri and Outlines	21-24
§6. Women's *'Awra* ('Nakedness')	25-32
§7. 'Tabarruj' – Displaying Charms (التبرج)	33-37
§8. The *Sunna* Aspects of Dress	38-39
§9. Some General Rulings	40-44
§10. The Politics of Clothing: *The Veil Controversy*	45-53
Key References	54-57

TABLE OF ABBREVIATIONS

Art.	=	article
Bk.	=	book
pp.	=	pages
ʾ	=	the Arabic letter ع
ʿ	=	the Arabic letter ء
ا. ه	=	'end of quote' where a cited textual segment in Arabic ends.
s:	=	additional comments made by the translator

TABLE OF SYMBOLS

#	=	*hadith* number
(…)	=	contains transliteration of Arabic terms
[…]	=	contains additions by the translator
… / […]	=	ellipsis where a textual segment is elided and omitted in translation by the translator
{…}	=	enclosure of a Qur'anic verse in translation
§	=	section

THE FIQH *of* CLOTHING *and* DRESS

الحمد لله حمداً يبلغ رضاه وصلى الله على أشرف من اجتباه وعلى من صاحبه ووالاه وسلم تسليماً لا يدرك منتهاه.

Praise be to Allah Most High; The Giver of this perfect and final Law for all times and abundant blessings upon our beloved Prophet, the Divine Mercy sent for humankind who embodied this perfect Law and implemented it for all to follow and who is the Light of guidance that has radiated the firmaments. Blessings too upon his noble companions who followed His blessed example in implementing this sacred law, his pure family and all those who follow them in creed and deed until the Final Day. ***To proceed***:

◆

§1. Introduction

Allah (swt) says in His Majestic Book:

{يَٰبَنِىٓ ءَادَمَ قَدْ أَنزَلْنَا عَلَيْكُمْ لِبَاساً يُوَارِي سَوْءَاتِكُمْ وَرِيشاً وَلِبَاسُ ٱلتَّقْوَىٰ ذَٰلِكَ خَيْرٌ ذَٰلِكَ مِنْ آيَاتِ ٱللَّهِ لَعَلَّهُمْ يَذَّكَّرُونَ}

{O children of Adam! Surely we have bestowed upon you a garment to cover your shame, as well as to be an adornment to you; and the garment of piety is the best}[1]

- Our law is sacred because it is From Allah (swt).[2]

- Our Sacred Law is the most perfect legal system because it is from Allah (swt).[3]

- Our Sacred Law has abrogated all previous legal systems and indeed our *din* has abrogated all earlier religions.[4]

- It is the view of all *usuli* scholars as well as theologians that the human mind (*'aql*) cannot

---

[1] See Q. 7:26. Ibn al-Jawzi comments on the verse: "And regarding Allah's saying: {**O children of Adam! Surely We have bestowed upon you a garment to cover your shame**}; the reason for its revelation is that the Arabs would circumambulate the House [s: i.e. the Ka'ba] naked so this verse came down in response to that. This is what Mujahid held…regarding the meaning of {**We have bestowed upon you**} there are three opinions: The first is that it means: 'We have created for you garments'. The second is that it means: 'We have shown you how to manufacture these garments' and the third is that it means: 'We have sent down the rain which causes plants to grow and from which you subsequently produce your garments.'" See *Zad al-Masir fi 'Ilm al-Tafsir*, 3:123.

وله تعالى: { يا بني آدم قد أنزلنا عليكم لباساً } سبب نزولها: أن ناساً من العرب كانوا يطوفون بالبيت عراةً، فنزلت هذه الآية، قاله مجاهد. وقيل: إنه لما ذكر عري آدم، منّ علينا باللباس. وفي معنى: { أنزلنا عليكم } ثلاثة أقوال. أحدها: خلقنا لكم. والثاني: ألهمناكم كيفية صنعه. والثالث: أنزلنا المطر الذي هو سبب نبات ما يتخذ لباساً

[2] Shah 'Abd al-Haqq al-Dihlawi, *Takmil al-Iman*, p.101.
[3] Shah 'Abd al-Haqq al-Dihlawi, *Takmil al-Iman*, p.101.
[4] Shah 'Abd al-Haqq al-Dihlawi, *Takmil al-Iman*, p.147.

ascertain what is right and what is wrong related to moral actions and indeed any action.[5]

- It is also the view of the scholars of *Usul al-Fiqh* (Islamic jurisprudence) that legal injunctions and rulings pertaining to food, clothing and drinks may often elude rational causes (*'illa*) and so the believer takes these on the utter conviction and trust that the Lawgiver – Allah (swt) – has legislated them in the general best interest of human beings and that there is wisdom (*hikam*) underpinning them.

- The same point extends to the blessed *sunna* (example) of humanity's greatest blessing (and indeed that of all creation) the beloved of Allah our beloved the Messenger of Allah (may the abundant peace and blessings of Allah be upon him).

- Hence, our immediate consternation of being unable to determine any sense or coherence upon coming to know the relevant legal injunctions and rulings does not warrant the inference that they neither have coherence nor are they practically enforceable. *We listen and we obey.*

- It is also our conviction that our legal tradition has been delineated by the greatest legal minds and personalities – arguably – unrivalled in any civilisation.

- We believe that our noble scholar-jurists (*mujtahidun* and *fuqaha'*) were:

    1. Trustworthy.
    2. Qualified.
    3. Pious.

---

[5] al-Nabhani, *al-Shakhsiyya al-Islamiyya*, 3:14-18.

4. Sincere.
5. But fallible.

- Moreover, we approach the study of the *fiqh* with humility and reverence but with a critical engagement of this legacy. And may Allah enable us to carry out the tasks required of us. *Amin.*

- This is a small booklet outlining some very basic legal injunctions and rulings pertaining to dress and clothing as found within the School (*madhhab*) of the noble Imam Abu Hanifa Nu'man ibn Thabit (80-150/768) – may Allah be pleased with him.[6] There is no extensive analysis nor are their comparative discussions and evaluations although some *fiqh* discussions are given of some common questions surrounding clothe types and contemporary realities. It is hoped that this small contribution helps those who read it and nothing is asked of them except sincere *du'as*.

---

[6] For some general biographical references on Imam Abu Hanifa in English, see art. "Abu Hanifa" by J. Schacht, 1:123 in EI^2 and H. Yanagihashi, "Abu Hanifa" in EI^3 and references therein; G. F. Haddad's extensive account in *The Four Imams and Their Schools* as well as Sh. Abu Zahra's chapter in *The Four Imams: Their Lives, Works and Schools of Thought*; A. Nadwi, *Abu Hanifa: His Life, Legal Method and Legacy*; the '*Uqud al-Jumman fi Manaqib Abi Hanifa al-Nu'man* of al-Salihi (tr. Madrasa Arabia Islamyyia S.A.) and Shibli Numani's *Imam Abu Hanifa: Life and Works* (tr. M. Hussain).

§2. Some Preliminary *Fiqh* Rules

- Below are some of the rules pertaining the *ahkam* (rulings) on dress and clothing (*libas*) in order to serve as a general guide:

Rule 1: Anything done out of pride is considered disliked (*tahriman* and *tanzihan*) and this includes wearing clothes:

و الحاصل أن كل ما فعل تجبرا كره...

"Whatever is done out of arrogance (*tajabburan*) is considered not allowed but if done out of need it is not..."[7]

Rule 2: Anything worn out of need is not considered disliked (*tahriman* and *tanzihan*) and this includes prohibited clothing items:

و الحاصل أن كل ما فعل تجبرا كره و ما فعل لحاجة لا...

"The point is that anything done out of arrogance and pride is disliked [s: prohibited] but anything done out of need is not..."[8]

و الحاصل أن كل ما كان على وجه التكبر يجره و إن فعل لحاجة و ضرورة لا و هو المختار إه .

"[...] but if something is done out of need or a necessity, then it is not unlawful and this is the preferred opinion..."[9]

---

[7] al-Haskafi, *Durr al-Mukhtar*, 6:363-364.
[8] Ibn 'Abidin, *Radd al-Muhtar*, 6:363.
[9] Ibn 'Abidin, *Radd al-Muhtar*, 6.363.

Rule 3: <u>Intentionally</u> imitating non-Muslims is not permissible and this includes dress, style and clothing:

وجوزه الشافعي بلا كراهة وهما بها للتشبه بأهل الكتاب : أي إن قصده؛ فإن التشبه بهم لا يكره في كل شيء، بل في المذموم وفيما يقصد به التشبه، كما في البحر...

"And al-Shafi'i permitted [s: recitation of the Qur'an from the noble *Mushaf*] without any dislike. However, both [s: Imam Abu Yusuf and Muhammad al-Shaybani] did not because it resembled the actions of the People of the Book – i.e. if the person intended to do so. Imitating non-Muslims is not disliked in everything but only in what is blameworthy and only if one intends to imitate them as mentioned in *al-Bahr*..."[10]

---

[10] Ibn 'Abidin, *Radd al-Muhtar*, 1:624:

مطلب في التشبه بأهل الكتاب (قوله لأن التشبه بهم لا يكره في كل شيء) فإنا نأكل ونشرب كما يفعلون بحر عن شرح الجامع الصغير لقاضي خان... قال هشام : رأيت على أبي يوسف نعلين مخصوفين بمسامير، فقلت : أترى بهذا الحديد بأسا؟ قال لا قلت : سفيان وثور بن يزيد كرها ذلك لأن فيه تشبها بالرهبان ؛ فقال { كان رسول الله صلى الله عليه وسلم يلبس النعال التي لها شعر } وإنها من لباس الرهبان. فقد أشار إلى أن صورة المشابهة فيما تعلق به صلاح العباد لا يضر، فإن الأرض مما لا يمكن قطع المسافة البعيدة فيها إلا بهذا النوع . ١ ه وفيه إشارة أيضا إلى أن المراد بالتشبه أصل الفعل : أي صورة المشابهة بلا قصد

"[..] (**And his saying that imitating them [s: the people of the Book] is not disliked in all matters**) is because we eat and drink just like they do as in *Bahr* from the *Sharh* of *al-Jami' al-Saghir* of Qadi Khan [...] Hisham said: I saw Abu Yusuf wearing sandals with curved metals on them and so I asked him: are you wearing these metal attachments out of distress? He replied: No. So I said to him: But Sufyan and Thawr b. Yazid have both discouraged this because it imitates what the non-Muslim monks wear. [Abu Yusuf] replied saying: The Prophet wore sandals with hair on it. [s: Ibn 'Abidin remarks: And that is what monks wear]. This point indicates that the appearance of resembling religious people is not harmful...In it is also an indication regarding imitation for

Rule 4: In origin, the ruling is that all objects are permissible unless specified not to be:

الأصل في الأشياء الإباحة حتى يدل الدليل على التحريم...

"**The legal norm is that**: All things and objects (e.g. food, clothes, utensils, drinks, etc.) are lawful until proven to the contrary through legal evidence. Therefore the operating assumption is that all objects not yet existent unless already prohibited are permitted unless legal evidence restricts their use, their consumption, usufruct or trade."[11]

---

the basis an action: it was an appearance of imitation without any intention to do so..."

[11] Sh. Wahba Zuhayli, *al-Qawa'id al-Fiqhiyya*, 1:189-192.

§3. Clothing Guidelines –
Imam Ibn 'Abidin

──────── ♦ ────────

- Imam Ibn 'Abidin commences the section on clothing (*libas*) in his *magnum opus* entitled *Radd al-Muhtar* on Hanafi legal rulings with the following section quoted from *al-Multaqa*:

"Know that covering the body can be:

[1] obligatory (*fard*) where the *'awra* is covered protecting from the heat or cold preferably with cotton, linen and wool in conformity with the *sunna* in that its bottom [s: lower end] trails as far as half the leg...

[2] prohibited (*nahy*) which is any clothing that emulates other religions and is mean and base;

[3] recommended (*mustahabb*) which is any additional thing in order to beautify and adorn oneself in order to show the bounty and blessing given my Allah because he (upon him be peace said): **'Allah loves to see the effects of His blessing on His servants'**;

[4] permitted (*mubah*) which

اعلم أن الكسوة منها فرض وهو ما يستر العورة ويدفع الحر والبرد، والأولى كونه من القطن أو الكتان أو الصوف على وفاق السنة بأن يكون ذيله لنصف ساقه وكمه لرؤوس أصابعه وفمه قدر شبر كما في النتف بين النفيس والخسيس، إذ خير الأمور أوساطها. وللنهي عن الشهرتين: وهو ما كان في نهاية النفاسة أو الخساسة. ومستحب: وهو الزائد لاخذ الزينة وإظهار نعمة الله تعالى، قال عليه الصلاة والسلام: إن الله يحب أن يرى أثر نعمته على عبده. ومباح: وهو الثوب الجميل للتزين في الأعياد والجمع ومجامع الناس لا في جميع الأوقات لأنه

is to wear beautiful clothes such as adorning oneself in the two 'Ids, Fridays and congregations but not all the time otherwise it borders on opulence and pomposity;

[5] disliked (*makruh*) which is wearing any item of clothing out of pride.

It is recommended to wear white or black because it is one of the signs of Banu 'Abbas. The Prophet (upon him be peace) entered Mecca with a black turban on his head. Wearing green is a *sunna* as mentioned in *al-Shir'a*...”[12]

- Imam Ibn 'Abidin continues elsewhere stating:

"(**His saying as long as you cannot describe what's underneath**) so that the skin of the underneath cannot be seen being careful it is not thin or transparent (**And his saying there is no harm if it touches**) ... and the wording in *Sharh al-Munya* is: if the [s: material] is thick [s: or coarse] such that the colour of the skin cannot be seen but it touches the body part making its shape

صلف وخيلاء، وربما يغيظ المحتاجين فالتحرز عنه أولى ومكروه وهو اللبس للتكبر، ويستحب الأبيض وكذا الأسود لأنه شعار بني العباس، ودخل عليه الصلاة والسلام مكة وعلى رأسه عمامة سوداء ولبس الأخضر سنة كما في الشرعة اه.

(قوله لا يصف ما تحته) بأن لا يرى منه لون البشرة احترازا عن الرقيق ونحو الزجاج (قوله ولا يضر التصاقه) أي بالألية مثلا، وقوله وتشكله من عطف المسبب على السبب. وعبارة شرح المنية: أما لو كان غليظا لا يرى منه لون

---

[12] Ibn 'Abidin, *Radd al-Muhtar*, 6:667.

appear visible such that the body part can be ascertained, then it does not prevent the prayer's validity because she has covered herself..."[13]

البشرة إلا أنه التصق بالعضو وتشكل بشكله فصار شكل العضو مرئيا فينبغي أن لا يمنع جواز الصلاة لحصول الستر ا

ه

- The above excerpt is a convenient summary for general guidelines of Islamic dress for both men and women and include:

1. **Concealing the body**: the extent for men includes from the naval to – and including – the knees and for women it encompasses her entire body excluding the hands and face in general.

2. **Appropriate materials**: the clothing cannot be thin, visible and transparent such that the private parts are visible or the colour of the skin (*lawn al-bashra*). This also includes the shape of the private parts and in the case of women, the chest and hips as well.

3. **No intentional imitation**: clothing must not imitate the non-Muslims or anything considered vile, mean, base, vulgar and degrading. It must also not imitate opposite gender clothing items.[14]

4. **Pomposity**: one should not wear clothes out of arrogance, extravagance, ostentation and pride.

5. **Pure/clean**: clothes must be free from *najasa* (نجاسة / 'filth') and dirt.

---

[13] Ibn 'Abidin, *Radd al-Muhtar*, 6:410.
[14] For a detailed discussion of the topic *tashabbuh* ('imitation') see s.v. "tashabbuh", *al-Mawsu'at al-Fiqhiyya*, 13:12-17.

If an item of clothing satisfies these conditions, it will be clothing that accords with Islamic standards.

§4. The Categories *of* Clothing

───── ♦ ─────

- It is helpful to tabularise the main areas on which the jurists have pronounced their legal rulings (examples are mainly equivalent contemporary items):

[1] Upper Garments:

- Shirts.
- T-shirts.
- Vests.
- Jumpers.
- Tunics.
- Gowns.
- Dresses.
- Shawls.
- Wraps.
- Jackets.
- Coats.
- Robes.
- Cloaks.
- Waist-coats.
- Bras.
- Qamis.

[2] Lower garments:

- Trousers.
- Pants.
- Leggings.
- Boxer shorts.
- Shorts.
- Knickers.
- Pants.
- Thongs.
- Three quarter lengths.

- Tights.
- Sarongs (lungis, etc.).
- Salwar.
- Jeans.

[3] Headgear:

- Hats.
- Skull caps.
- Turbans.
- Hoods.

[4] Footwear

- Shoes.
- Sandals.
- Slippers.
- Socks.
- Boots.
- High-heels.
- Flip-flops.

- In addition to the above areas of dress and clothing, there is also the clothing *accessory*, i.e. those items that augment, beautify and make clothes versatile such as:

1. Canes.
2. Hats.
3. Scarves.
4. Gloves.
5. bags
6. Watches.
7. Jewellery (anklets, bracelets, earring, rings, etc.).
8. Belts.
9. Straps.

10. Wigs.
11. Glasses.
12. Pins.
13. Stockings.
14. Tights.
15. Leggings.
16. Pins.
17. Ties.
18. Cuff links.

- All the above items are in general permissible to use and wear.

- General items of clothing the scholars have mentioned and discussed in their legal works include:

    1) *Jubba* (gowns).
    2) *Na'al* (sandals).
    3) *Sarawil* (trousers).
    4) *Qulunsuwa* (hats, skull-caps).
    5) *Qubba* (coat).
    6) *Izar* (sarong, waist cloth).
    7) *Kasrawani* (tunics, sherwanis).
    8) *Qamis* (shirts and tunics).
    9) *Tikka* (drawstring, tousle).

- General fabrics the scholars have also discussed and considered permitted include for example:

Qatn	= cotton.
Kattan	= linen.
Suf	= wool.
Jild; julud	= leather skin.
Ibraysim	= fine silk fabric.
Kirbas	= muslin cotton.

Khazz = silky fabric

- In general therefore, considering all the above, all items of clothing and accessory are assumed permitted to wear with the exception of the following:

[1] Clothing items linked to a specific, religion or ideology:	[2] Clothing prohibited by text (*nusus*):	[3] Clothing that does not cover the '*awra*:
- Liturgical garments (e.g. vestments). - Religious robes (Christian, Jewish, Hindu, other...).	- Silk clothing (*al-harir*) for men. - Wearing full red coloured clothing or items.[16]	- Ripped/seared jeans along frontal and rear area. - Mini-skirts. - Hot-pants. - Short skirts.

---

[16] The Hanafi *fuqaha'* have ruled that it is permissible to wear red coloured clothes as there are narrations that explicitly mention the Prophet doing so. Ibn 'Abidin concludes the following:

(قوله لا بأس بلبس الثوب الأحمر) وقد روي ذلك عن الإمام كما في الملتقط ا هـ ط (قوله ومفاده أن الكراهة تنزيهية) لأن كلمة لا بأس تستعمل غالبا فيما تركه أولى منح ...

"(**And his saying there is no problem in wearing red**) which was mentioned from the Imam [s: Abu Hanifa] as in *al-Multaqat*. (**His saying that it implies slight dislike [*karaha tanzihiyya*]**) is because the phrase 'there is no problem' (*la ba's*) is used mainly to refer to leaving things as the preferred action..." *Radd al-Muhtar*, 6:358 and cf. Imam Zafar Usmani, *I'la' al-Sunan*, 17:38-360 for a discussion.

- Religious headgears (e.g. skull caps, etc.).

- Talismans.

- Cassocks.

- Cardinal collars.

- Crosses.

- Communist hammer and sickle.[15]

- Clothes dyed with saffron.[17]

- Swim-suits.

- Bikinis.

- Tank tops, etc.

---

[15] However, if the item of clothing passes out of being specifically linked to that religious tradition or ideology, then it will become a permissible item of clothing to wear:

وإنما يصلح الاستدلال بقصة اليهود في الوقت الذي تكون الطيالسة من شعارهم، وقد ارتفع ذلك في هذه الأزمنة فصار داخلا في عموم المباح...

"From the account of the Jew and the robe (*tayalis*) in its time being one of the signs [s: in their religion and culture] it would be valid to deduce that if this [s: robe] no longer is considered part of their religion and culture, it would fall in the generality of permissible things..." See al-Hafiz Ibn Hajar al-'Asqalani, *Fath al-Bari*, 10:274.

[17] Tirmidhi, *al-Shama'il* (#64). See *al-Muhit al-Burhani*, 8:42:

و في المنتقى : كان ابو حنيفة يكره للرجال ان يلبس الثوب المصغر بالمعصفر او بالورس و الزعفران للاثر الوارد فيه

See also *Fatawa Qadi Khan*, 3:315:

و يكره للرجال ان يلبس الثوب المصبوغ بالعصفر و الزعفران و الورس

§5. Imam al-Quduri and Outlines

◆

- Below is the textual segment from Imam al-Quduri's legal primer entitled *al-Mukhtasar* ('The Abridgment') on a number of general rulings pertaining to clothing:

"It is not permitted for men to wear silk (*al-harir*) although it is permitted for women.[18] There is no problem in using silk as a pillow (*tawassud*) according to Abu Hanifa but Abu Yusuf and Muhammad [al-Shaybani] considered it disliked.[19]	لا يحل للرجال لبس الحرير ويحل للنساء ولا بأس بتوسده عند أبي حنيفة وقال أبو يوسف ومحمد : يكره توسده ولا بأس بلبس الديباج في الحرب عندهما ويكره عند أبي حنيفة

---

[18] Imam al-Ghunaymi (= 'Abd al-Ghani al-Nabulusi) in his commentary on the *Mukhtasar* of Imam al-Quduri mentions:

إلا إذا كان قدر أربع أصابع كما في القنية وغيرها وفيها : عمامة طرزها قدر أربع أصابع من إبريسم من أصابع عمر رضي الله تعالى عنه وذلك قيس بشبرنا يرخص فيه اه . وكذا الثوب المنسوج بذهب يحل إذا كان هذا المقدار وإلا لا كما في الزيلعي وغيره...

"If it is 4 finger lengths, then it is permitted to wear silk as mentioned in *al-Qunya* and other works: 'a turban woven from silky *ibraysim* fabric a total of 4 finger lengths – the size of 'Umar's (see Bukhari, *Sahih* [#5828] and Muslim, *Sahih* [#2069]) – and that is analogous to a hand span as an exemption'. The same holds for clothes woven with a texture of gold. It would be permitted if it was 4 finger lengths otherwise it would not be as in al-Zayla'i and others." See *al-Lubab*, 3:213.

[19] Because Imam Abu Hanifa saw it as a form of debasing (*istikhfaf*) like sitting on images etched on rugs and carpets. al-Ghunaymi, *al-Lubab*, 3:213:

لأن ذلك استخفاف به فصار كالتصاوير على البساط فإنه يجوز الجلوس عليه ولا يجوز لبس التصاوير اختيار...

There is no objection to wearing silk brocades (*al-daybaj*) in war according to both [Abu Yusuf and Muhammad] although Abu Hanifa considered it disliked.

There is no problem in wearing woven clothes (*mulham*) when its [s: threads = warp] is silk and its weft is either cotton or a silky fabric (*khazz*).

It is not permitted for men to wear jewellery (*al-tahalli*) made of gold or silver except for a ring, belt or a sword with silver decorations.

It is permitted for women to wear jewellery made of gold and silver.

It is disliked for a young male minor (*sabi*) to be dressed in gold and silk.[20]

ولا بأس بلبس الملحم إذا كان سداه إبريسيما ولحمته قطنا أو خزا

ولا يجوز للرجال التحلي بالذهب والفضة إلا الخاتم والمنطقة وحلية السيف من الفضة

ويجوز للنساء التحلي بالذهب والفضة .

ويكره أن يلبس الصبي الذهب والحرير

ولا يجوز الأكل والشرب والادهان والتطيب في آنية الذهب والفضة للرجال والنساء

ولا بأس باستعمال آنية الزجاج والبلور والعقيق

ويجوز الشرب في الإناء المفضض عند أبي حنيفة والركوب على السرج المفضض

"Because to do that in reality is to debase it and so it becomes like in the case of pictures on carpets and mats. It is permitted to sit on them although it is not permitted to wear anything with pictures on them..."

[20] A guardian of a child should steer and guide the child to the Shari'a rulings and nurture in them an affinity for it. *al-Lubab*, 3:214:

لأن التحريم لما ثبت في حق الذكور وحرم اللباس حرم الإلباس كالخمر لما حرم شربه حرم سقيه ولأنه يجب عليه أن يعود الصبي طريق الشريعة ليألفها كالصوم والصلاة...

"[...] this is because [s: the guardian] must bring the child into line with the Shari'a so he becomes accustomed to it like in the case with Prayer and fasting..."

It is not permitted for men and women to eat, drink, apply oil or perfume from utensils and items made from gold and silver.[21]	والجلوس على السرير المفضض
	ويكره التعشير في المصحف والنقط
There is no problem in using utensils and items made of glass, lead, crystal and carnelian.[22]	ولا بأس بتحلية المصحف ونقش المسجد وزخرفته بماء الذهب
It is permitted according to Abu Hanifa to drink from a silver-plated vessel, as well as to mount a silver-plated saddle and sit on a silver-plated bed[23] […]"[24]	

Summary points from the text:

1. Men may not wear silk although women are permitted to wear it.

2. A silk pillow may be used according to Abu Hanifa but not his students Abu Yusuf and Muhammad al-Shaybani.

---

[21] This applies to all forms of utensils and objects for use because of the generality of the texts.
[22] Because they do not fall under the meaning of 'gold' and 'silver'. See al-Ghunaymi, *al-Lubab*, 3:214.
[23] This extends to all items that are plated whether on clothes or accessories. al-Ghunaymi, *al-Lubab*, 3:214. And this is the preferred opinion in the School.
[24] al-Quduri, *al-Mukhtasar*, pp.689-691 (= English) and al-Ghunaymi, *al-Lubab*, 3:212-216.

3. Men may wear silk brocades (woven patterns on a fabric) for war according to Abu Yusuf and Muhammad al-Shaybani but not Abu Hanifa who considered it disliked.

4. Wearing clothes that that have threaded silk is permitted or a weft that it is of silky fabric.

5. Men may not wear gold.

6. Men may not wear silver except if it is a ring or a belt or sword decorated in silver.

7. Women may wear silver and gold jewellery.

8. It is disliked for a minor to be dressed in gold and silver.

9. Using gold and silver utensils for eating and containing items are not permitted.

10. It is permitted to use a silver-platted vessel to eat from.

11. It is permitted to mount a silver-plated saddle.

§6. Women's *'Awra* ('Nakedness')

———— ♦ ————

- The legal manuals have large sections on what body parts it is permitted to look at (§.نظ / *nazar*). Often it is connected with rulings pertaining to where male gazes may extend to and where it may not in relation to women.

- Thus, the rulings connected to where it is permitted to look upon relate to whether or not that specific area is legally mandatory to cover. This is the discussion on *'awra*.

- Linguistically, the word <عورة / *'awra*> - from the root ' / w / r / - means 'to conceal one's nakedness'; 'a hidden place'; 'a blind spot' and 'anything that arouses shame when exposed'.[25]

- According to the legal meaning, it is those parts of the body that have to be covered with the appropriate clothing.[26]

- There are generally two sets of rulings with regards to women's *'awra* or covering (*satr*):

[1] scenario when performing the Prayer and

[2] scenario when not performing the Prayer.

- In the case of performing the Prayer, a woman's covering (*satr*) includes:

---

[25] See Ibn Manzur, *Lisan al-'Arab*, 9:370 and E. W. Lane, *Arabic-English Lexicon*, Bk.1, pp.2193-2195.
[26] Qal'aji, *Mu'jam al-Fiqh al-Luhga*, s.v. "'awra", p.293.

(1) The head such that not even one hair is visible and

(2) Full body (including the lower shin area) but not her hands, face and feet (according to Imam Abu Hanifa):[27]

(و) الرابع (ستر عورته) وللحرة جميع بدنها خلا الوجه والكفين والقدمين

(وللحرة) و لو خنثى (جميع بدنها) حتى شعرها النازل في الأصح (خلا الوجه والكفين) فظهر الكف عورة على المذهب (والقدمين) على المعتمد، وصوتها على الراجح وذراعيها على المرجوح...

"(**And for a free woman**) even if she is a hermaphrodite (**covering extends to her entire body**) even her hair that falls down over her face and sides according to the most correct position (**except the face and hands ...and the feet**) which is the relied upon position and includes her voice according to the strongest position as well as her forearms according to the less stronger position..."[28]

- In the case of when not performing Prayer, there are a number of realities regarding covering which have specific rulings:

---

[27] See *al-Bahr al-Ra'iq* of Ibn Nujaym, 1:467:

وحد الستر أن لا يرى ما تحته حتى لو سترها بثوب رقيق يصف ما تحته لا يجوز

al-Zayla'i. *Tabyin al-Haqa'iq*, 1:252:

والثوب الرقيق الذي يصف ما تحته لا تجوز الصلاة فيه؛ لأنه مكشوف العورة

[28] al-Haskafi, *Durr al-Muhkhtar*, 6:406 (= *Radd al-Muhtar*).

[1] In seclusion (*khalwa*):	[2] In the presence of one's husband:	[3] In the presence of Muslim women and non-Muslim women:
Her whole body should be (i) in full covering as it is consideration of required *adab* in modesty or (ii) cover minimally from the navel to the knees.[29]	Each may see the entire naked body of the other. However it is better to remain covered out of required courtesy (*adab*) to modesty.[30]	Minimally, she must cover from her navel to – and including – her knees, back and stomach if it does not provoke desire (*shahwa*).[31]

---

[29] Unless there is a valid reason like showering, relieving oneself, changing, sex, etc. However, one should still attempt to do this with minimal exposure:

(و) الرابع (ستر عورته) ووجوبه عام ولو في الخلوة على الصحيح إلا لغرض صحيح... (قوله والرابع ستر عورته) أي ولو بما لا يحل لبسه كثوب حرير وإن أثم بلا عذر، كالصلاة في الأرض المغصوبة، وسيذكر شروط الستر والساتر (قوله ووجوبه عام) أي في الصلاة وخارجها (قوله ولو في الخلوة) أي إذا كان خارج الصلاة يجب الستر بحضرة الناس إجماعا وفي الخلوة على الصحيح . وأما لو صلى في الخلوة عريانا ولو في بيت مظلم وله ثوب طاهر لا يجوز إجماعا كما في البحر. ثم إن الظاهر أن المراد بما يجب ستره في الخلوة خارج الصلاة هو ما بين السرة والركبة فقط، حتى إن المرأة لا يجب عليها ستر ما عدا ذلك وإن كان عورة يدل عليه ما في باب الكراهية من القنية، حيث قال : وفي غريب الرواية يرخص للمرأة كشف الرأس في منزلها وحدها فأولى لها لبس خمار رقيق يصف ما تحته عند محارمها ا ه

"(And) the fourth condition (is covering the '*awra*) which is mandatory in all situations even in *khalwa* according to the most correct understanding unless it is for a valid and sound reason [...] (His saying the fourth condition is covering up...even in *khalwa*) [...] refers to when external to the Prayer because of the presence of other people according to consensus and in *khalwa* according to the most correct

Again, consideration to modesty is paramount.

In the presence of non-Muslim women, she must be in full covering.[32]

---

position [...] and covering up when external to the Prayer is from the navel and the knees which is also for women; hence it is not mandatory for her to cover more than these two [s: i.e. the navel and the knees]..." al-Haskafi, *Durr al-Mukhtar* as in Ibn 'Abidin's *Radd al-Muhtar*, 1:404.

[30] For a discussion, see this author's book *Introducing the Fiqh of Marital Intimacy*, pp.12-24.

[31] In al-Haskafi's *Durr al-Mukhtar* it states:

(وتنظر المرأة المسلمة من المرأة كالرجل من الرجل) و قيل كالرجل لمحرمه والأول أصح سراج (وكذا) تنظر المرأة (من الرجل) كنظر الرجل للرجل (إن أمنت شهوتها) فلو لم تأمن أو خافت أو شكت حرم استحسانا...

"(**A Muslim woman looking at another woman takes the same ruling as whatever one is allowed to look at in another man**). It is also said that it is the case of what a man may see of his *mahram* although the first is more correct as in *Siraj*. (**Likewise**) a woman may look at (**in a man**) whatever a man may see of another man (**if it is not out of sexual desire**). If the woman is not free from sexual desire, or if she fears or doubts [s: herself] it is unlawful based on *istihsan*..." Ibn 'Abidin's commentary further down mentions:

[32] However, there is a difference of opinion over this amongst scholars. However, the position of the Hanafi School as unequivocally stated by Ibn 'Abidin in *Radd al-Muhtar*, 6:371 is that it is not permitted:

(قوله فلا تنظر إلخ) قال في غاية البيان : وقوله تعالى { - أو نسائهن - } أي الحرائر المسلمات، لأنه ليس للمؤمنة أن تتجرد بين يدي مشركة أو كتابية ا ه ونقله في العناية وغيرها عن ابن عباس، فهو تفسير مأثور وفي شرح الأستاذ عبد الغني النابلسي على هدية ابن العماد عن شرح والده الشيخ إسماعيل على الدرر والغرر : لا

[4]	[5]	[6]
In the presence of *mahram* males.	**In front of non-*mahram* males:**	**In front of non-Muslim *mahram* males:**
Mahram (محرم) = Father, brother, uncle, son, paternal uncle, maternal uncle, step-sons, grandfather, son-in-law, etc...[33]	*Ghayr mahram* (غير محرم) such as [1] brother-in-law, [2] cousin	In front of non-Muslim *mahram* males and females, the ruling is that of [4] because: • There is no

---

يحل للمسلمة أن تنكشف بين يدي يهودية أو نصرانية أو مشركة إلا أن تكون أمة لها كما في السراج، ونصاب الاحتساب ولا تنبغي للمرأة الصالحة أن تنظر إليها المرأة الفاجرة لأنها تصفها عند الرجال، فلا تضع جلبابها ولا خمارها كما في السراج ا هـ

"**(His statement she may not look at...)** It is mentioned in *Ghayat al-Bayan*: Allah's statement {*or their womenfolk*...} means their free believing women because a believing woman should not undress [s: expose herself] in front of polytheists and People of the Book. It is mentioned in *al-'Inaya* and other works from Ibn 'Abbas; a narrational exegesis of 'Abd al-Ghani al-Nabulusi's commentary on the *Hadiyya* of Ibn al-'Imad from his father's commentary Shaykh Isma'il 'Ali on *al-Durar* and *al-Ghurar* that: it is not permitted for a believing woman to uncover herself in front of Jewish and Christian as well as polytheist womenfolk unless it is her own salve-girl as in *al-Siraj*...And a pious woman ought not to let an impious woman look at her as she may describe her to other men. Hence, she should not take off her *jilbab* (long robe/drape) and *khimar* (headscarf) as mentioned in *al-Siraj*..."

[33] Imam al-Kasani states in *al-Bada'i' al-Sana'i'*, 2:124:

ُمَّ صِفَةُ الْمَحْرَمِ أَنْ يَكُونَ مِمَّنْ لَا يَجُوزُ لَهُ نِكَاحُهَا عَلَى التَّأْبِيدِ إِمَّا بِالْقَرَابَةِ أَوِ الرَّضَاعِ أَوِ الصِّهْرِيَّةِ...

In front of them, she may expose:

(i) head,

(ii) hair,

(iii) face,

(iv) shoulders,

(v) chest (including her breast area),[34]

brother,

[3] paternal uncles,

[3] maternal uncles,

[4] husband's uncles,

[5] husband's nephews, etc.[37]

In the presence of

textual qualification (*taqyid*) that a *mahram* has to be Muslim.

- Because a woman may perform Hajj with the company of a non-Muslim *mahram* man.

"The description of a *mahram* is that person with whom marriage is not permitted because of a permanent relationship such as through kinship, suckling or through marriage..."

[34] Imam Ibn 'Abidin mentions in *Radd al-Muhtar*, 1:404-405 on the discussion of whether or not the chest and breast are part of the *'awra*:

(قوله مع ظهرها وبطنها) البطن: ما لان من المقدم، والظهر ما يقابله من المؤخر كذا في الخزائن . وقال الرحمتي :الظهر ما قابل البطن من تحت الصدر إلى السرة جوهرة : أي فما حاذى الصدر ليس من الظهر الذي هو عورة . ا هـ . ومقتضى هذا أن الصدر وما قابله من الخلف ليس من العورة وأن الثدي أيضا غير عورة وسيأتي في الحظر والإباحة أنه يجوز أن ينظر من أمة غيره ما ينظر من محرمه، ولا شبهة أنه يجوز النظر إلى صدر محرمه وثديها، فلا يكون عورة منها ولا من الأمة، ومقتضى ذلك أنه لا يكون عورة في الصلاة أيضا، لكن في التاترخانية : لو صلت الأمة ورأسها مكشوفة جازت بالاتفاق، ولو صلت وصدرها وثديها مكشوف لا يجوز عند أكثر مشايخنا . ا هـ

"(**And his saying in addition to her back and stomach**). The meaning of the 'stomach' is: the soft area from the front and the 'back' is its opposite from the rear' as mentioned in *al-Khaza'in*. al-Rahmati states: the 'back' is what is parallel to the 'stomach from below the chest (*sadr*) until the navel (*surra*) as in *Jawhara*. Thus, whatever is opposite [s: parallel] to the chest is not considered to be within what is the back area which is *'awra*.' What this necessitates is that the chest and its opposite from the rear are not considered part of the *'awra*. Her breasts are not considered part of the *'awra* either. In the section on 'Permissions and Prohibitions there will be an explanation on where it is allowed to look at

(vi) forearms,

(vii) hands,

(viii) shin.

She may **not** expose:

(a) her stomach area (and its sides),

(b) back area (and its sides)[35] and

(c) the area between the navel and knees,

(d) cleavage (if it generates *fitna*).[36]

ghayr mahram males she must have full covering like for the Prayer, i.e. the whole body except the hands and face.

---

the slave girl (*ama*) and other *mahram* women. There is no doubt that it is permitted to look at the chest and breast of the *mahram* women as it is not part of her '*awra* nor that of a slave-girl..."

[37] Those male individuals the law legally permits marriage to.

[35] It is stated in *al-Qunya* of Imam al-Zahidi that:

قال في القنية : الجنب تبع البطن، ثم رمز وقال : الأوجه أن ما يلي البطن تبع له، وما يلي الظهر تبع له ا هـ

"It is mentioned in *al-Qunya*: the side takes the ruling of the stomach. He then annotated and said: what is most clear is that whatever follows the stomach takes its ruling and whatever follows the back takes its rulings..." Ibn 'Abidin, *Radd al-Muhtar*, 1:406.

[36] The general ruling is that whatever is permitted to be seen is permitted to remain uncovered and to be touched:

However, additional consideration of modesty should always prevail.

- **Caveat**: this is a strict legal pronouncement of the Jurists of the Hanafi School of what the law minimally does not consider to be legal/illegal or lawful/unlawful. Context, prudence and circumstance may determine adoption of stricter or cautionary rulings.

وَأَمَّا نَظَرُهُ إِلَى ذَوَاتِ مَحَارِمِهِ فَنَقُولُ يُبَاحُ له أَنْ يَنْظُرَ مِنها إِلَى مَوْضِعِ زِينَتِهَا الظَّاهِرَةِ وَالْبَاطِنَةِ وَهِيَ الرَّأْسُ وَالشَّعْرُ وَالْعُنُقُ وَالصَّدْرُ وَالْأُذُنُ وَالْعَضُدُ وَالسَّاعِدُ وَالْكَفُّ وَالسَّاقُ وَالرِّجْلُ وَالْوَجْهُ...

"As for what is permitted for him to look at from those prohibited to him in marriage, we say and permit him the following parts to look at that are areas of overt and apparent adornment as well as non-apparent adornment: [1] the head, [2] hair, [3] neck, [4] chest, [5] ears, [6] shoulders, [7] forearm , [8] hands, [9] shins, [10] feet and [11] face..." Ibn al-Nizam et al, *al-Fatawa al-Hindiyya*, 5:328.

§7. "al-Tabarruj..." – Displaying Charms

- Shaykh 'Ata' b. Khalil (Allah protect him) responds to a question on the notion of "*tabarruj*" (التبرج) and explains it as follows:[38]

Answer: 5. "It should be known that '*tabarruj*' is displaying adornments (*zina*) in a way that attracts the attention [s: or the look of a person] without uncovering the private part ('*awra*). This specification – viz. 'without uncovering the '*awra* – is made because displaying adornments by uncovering the '*awra* is unlawful (*haram*) regardless of whether or not it attracts attention.

The point [s: of *tabarruj*] is not related to uncovering the '*awra* in like adorning her face [s: e.g. with make-up] or fingers [s: like with nail polish] or adorning her head-scarf (*khimar*) and body gown (*jilbab*) or her leg under her *jilbab* with for example anklets (*al-khalkhal*). All this type of *zina* if it is not customary in a town [s: or place] where a woman moves

خامساً: أعرف أن التبرج هو الزينة التي تلفت النظر، وعليه فإذا كان الخمار صغيراً وظهر شيء من شعر المرأة أو عنقها، هل تكون متبرجة؟ علماً أن هذا الجزء الصغير الظاهر من شعرها أو عنقها لا يلفت النظر، حيث إن كثيراً من النساء حاسرات الرأس بشكل معتاد في الشارع وأصبح ذلك لا يلفت النظر؟

الجواب: التبرج: هو إبداء الزينة بشكل لافت للنظر دون انكشاف العورة. وهذا القيد دون انكشاف العورة وُضع لأن الزينة مع انكشاف العورة حرام سواء لفتت النظر أم لَم تلفت.

فالموضوع هو في غير انكشاف العورة كأن تتزين على وجهها أو أصابعها أو تتزين بخمارها أو جلبابها، أو تتزين على ساقها تحت جلبابها كاللاتي يلبسن الخلخال ... فكل هذه الزينة إذا كانت غير معتادة في الوسط الذي تتحرك فيه

---

[38] See Sh. 'Ata' b. Khalil, "Q.5. al-Tabarruj".

about and if it is displayed in a way that attracts the attention, it would be designated as 'tabarruj' and would therefore be considered *haram*.

If a woman from a specific village (*qarya*) for example were to adorn her fingernails and it was not customary [s: in such a village] for such a thing to be seen, then such a type of *zina* draws the attention of others it would be considered *tabarruj* and *haram* even though the hand is not '*awra*. If [s: as another example] she were to strike her feet on the ground such that the sound of her anklets can be heard and it draws attention to the adornment on her leg, then even if her leg is covered, this would be considered *tabarruj* and thus *haram*. If she were to wear a *khimar*, unusual and uncustomary like brocaded and decorated such that it draws attention to her, this would not be permitted even if her hair was [s: completely] covered. And again, if she were to wear a *jilbab* with designs on the chest that attracted the attention of others, that would be considered *tabarruj* and is *haram* even though she is wearing an Islamic dress.

<u>In summary then</u>: any form of *zina* that draws attention (without uncovering the '*awra*) is *tabarruj* and is *haram*. Any form of *zina* that involves uncovering the '*awra* is *haram* regardless of whether or not it attracts attention. Uncovering the '*awra* is *haram* anyway.

Therefore, any form of *zina* that attracts the gaze as we have explained it is *tabarruj* and that is not allowed. And [*tabarruj*] is known through the circumstances and contexts of that town where a woman lives in and which is not difficult to ascertain because both men and women can determine that and recognise it [...]

Allah Glorified is He says {**and do not show your *zina* except for what is apparent from them...**} and 'whatever is apparent' (*ma zahar minha*) is interpreted by Ibn 'Abbas as being the face and hands...''[39]

---

[39] See al-Tabari, *al-Jami' al-Bayan*, 22:4; al-Zamakhshari, *al-Kashshaf*, 3:425; al-Baydawi, *Anwar al-Tanzil*, 2:128 and Ibn Kathir, *Tafsir al-Qur'an al-'Azim*, 3:482-483. Cf. al-Nabhani, *Nizam al-Ijtima'i fi'l-Islam*, pp.65-66.

... الآية} و(ما ظهر منها) أي الوجه والكفان كما فسرها ابن عباس رضي الله عنهما، ويقول الرسول صلى الله عليه وسلم «إن الجارية إذا حاضت لم يصلح أن يرى منها إلا وجهها ويداها إلى المفصل» أخرجه أ. داود، فغير الوجه والكفين يحرم على المرأة أن تكشفه لغير الزوج والمحارم وفق الأدلة.

لذلك فإن الواجب هو لبس الخمار الكافي لغطاء الشعر والعنق ولويه على الصدر بحيث لا يظهر إلا الوجه والكفان. يقول تعالى {وليضربن بخمرهن على جيوبهن} أي تلوي الخمار على (الجيب) وهو فتحة القميص حتى لا يظهر العنق، فيكون غطاء لكل من الرأس والأذن والعنق إلا الوجه والكفين فيجوز أن يظهرا من جسمها.

Thus, from the above:

- The general meaning of *tabarruj* is "making apparent and obvious one's adornments (*zina*) and beauties (*mahasin*) to a stranger".[40]

- It involves drawing attention, i.e. the gaze or attraction of someone either by strutting about, swaggering, showing adornments to attract or public display of charms/beauties, flaunting and wanton display of female beauty by which the sexual instinct

---

[40] al-Nabhani, *Nizam al-Ijtima'i fi'l-Islam*, p.98.

is agitated.[41] Thus, *tabarruj* is in both behaviour and appearance.

- *Tabarruj* can occur even if a woman is covered (i.e. it is not related to uncovering one's private parts) and even if she is in her own home (as there can be unrelated guests presents).[42] Otherwise the term is not applied when in front of her husband, parents and *mahrams*.

- *Tabarruj* is unlawful.[43]

- The idea of *tabarruj* is linked to the customs of a place (*'adat*).[44]

- The occurrence of *tabarruj* revolves around whether or not clothing in that context counts as 'drawing attention', 'attracting', 'enticing', 'luring', etc.

- From this it follows that: what is considered *tabarruj* may differ in different cultures and locations.

---

[41] al-Nabhani, *Nizam al-Ijtima'i fi'l-Islam*, p.99.
[42] al-Nabhani, *Nizam al-Ijtima'i fi'l-Islam*, p.98.
[43] al-Nabhani, *Nizam al-Ijtima'i fi'l-Islam*, p.98.
[44] al-Nabhani, *Nizam al-Ijtima'i fi'l-Islam*, p.98.

§8. The *Sunna* Aspects of Dress[45]

———— ♦ ————

Below are some of the aspects related to the blessed *sunnah* of the Prophet (saw):

- He would begin to dress from the right.[46]

- He liked wearing a long shirt up to his wrist but not over (perhaps akin to contemporary Asian kurtas).[47]

- His shirts used to have a collar line towards his noble chest.

- His shirts used to extend over the knee to above the ankles (which is interpreted as being halfway above his calf area).[48]

- He would wear a single sheet loin-cloth or a waist wrap (akin to sarongs).

- On one occasion he wore pants.[49]

- He would wear a head cap/skull cap often white in collar.[50]

- He would wear a turban (*'imama*) – sometimes black.

- He liked striped colours on colours.

---

[45] See also, Tirmidhi, *al-Shama'il* (#53-68).
[46] Abu Dawud, *Sunan* (#4141).
[47] Tirmidhi, *Sunan*, 1:306.
[48] al-Munawi, *Fayd al-Qadir*, 5:173.
[49] Mahmud Hasan Gangohi, *al-Fatawa al-Mahmudiyya*, 19:275.
[50] Mulla 'Ali al-Qari, *Mirqat al-Mafatih*, 8:246 and al-Haythami, *Majma' al-Zawa'id*, 5:21.

- He wore different colours such as black, green, red and preferred white.[51]

- He never wore one shoe or looked dishevelled but always encouraged cleanliness without it leading to pride and arrogance.[52]

- He never threw away clothes until they were patched and worn by him.

- He wore lower garments above the ankles.[53]

- He wore strapped sandals.

- He wore leather footgear.[54]

- He would put on clothes and praise Allah (swt).[55]

- On attaining new clothes, he would offer 2 *rak'at* Prayer of gratitude (*shukr*) and donate his old clothes to the poor.[56]

---

[51] Tirmidhi, *Sunan*, (#994).
[52] Muslim, *Sahih* (#91).
[53] Tirmidhi, *al-Shama'il* (#112-115).
[54] Tirmidhi, *al-Shama'il* (#69-70).
[55] Tirmidhi, *al-Shama'il* (#59).
[56] Tirmidhi, *Sunan* (#1767) and Abu Dawud, *Sunan* (#4020).

§9. Some General Rulings

──────── ♦ ────────

1. **Wearing earrings**: It is not permitted for men to wear ear-rings for a number of reasons: [1] men are only permitted to adorn themselves with a silver ring as an item of jewellery.[57] [2] Earrings are an item worn by women and hence it would be considered imitation of women's jewellery and adornment which is not permitted for men to do. [3] Earrings are an item worn by non-Muslim men and hence it would be considered imitation of non-Muslim adornment practices which is not permitted for men to do. [4] Any form of body modification is not permitted and ear piercing falls under such an action.

2. **Wearing the *niqab* ('veil')**: It is not mandatory for a Muslim woman to cover her face with a veil. However, there is a minor difference of opinion on this among the jurists.[58]

---

[57] Ibn 'Abidin, *Radd al-Muhtar*, 6:358-359:

قوله (ولا يتختم إلا بالفضة) هذه عبارة الإمام محمد في الجامع الصغير...(فيحرم بغيرها إلخ) لما روى الطحاوي بإسناده إلى عمران بن حصين وأبي هريرة قال نهى رسول الله صلى الله تعالى عليه وسلم عن خاتم الذهب وفي الجوهرة والتختم بالحديد والصفر والنحاس والرصاص مكروه للرجال والنساء...

"And his saying (**And he may only wear a silver ring**) which is Imam Muhammad's words in *al-Jami' al-Saghir*... (**and anything else is prohibited**) because of what al-Tahawi mentioned with his *isnad* to 'Imran b. Husayn and Abu Hurayra who said: The Messenger of Allah (saw) forbade gold rings and in *al-Jawhara* it has iron rings, brass, copper and led rings are disliked for men and women..."

[58] For the textual evidences as to why the face veil (*niqab*) is not mandatory, see al-Nabhani, *Nizam al-Ijtima'i fi 'l-Islam*, pp.54-70 and for discussions on the female dress, especially the veil, with contextual considerations for contemporary Muslims in Europe, see A. S. Roald,

3. **Imitation jewellery**: It is permitted for women to wear imitation jewellery.

4. **Wearing makeup**: it is permitted for women to adorn and beautify themselves with makeup for their husbands only but not in the presence of non-*mahram* men.

5. **Wearing a saree**: It is not permitted to wear a saree in the presence of anyone whether *mahram* or non-*mahram* except one's husband for the simple reason that the item of clothing does not cover the stomach and back which is *'awra*. If it is does, it will be permitted, strictly speaking, to wear it only in front of *mahram* males.

6. **Wearing a ring**: it is permitted for men to wear a ring made of silver only equivalent to 4.374 grams.[59]

7. **Haircuts**: For knowing what is a permissible type/style of haircut or not, the following account serves as a broad guideline:

    a. *Partially shaved head* (*qaz'* / قزع): this is impermissible (e.g. mowhawks, fohawk, half-shaves, patterned shave, extreme crew cut, etc.). This is based on the narration of Ibn 'Umar (ra) that "...the Messenger of Allah (saw) prohibited us from *qaza'*. Ibn Nafi' enquired: 'what is *qaza'*?' He replied: **"To**

Women In Islam: The Western Experience, pp.254-295 and K. Bullock, *Rethinking Muslim Women and the Veil*, pp.85-135.
[59] Ibn 'Abidin, *Radd al-Muhtar*, 6:359:

و لا يتحتم الا بالفضة لحصول الاستغناء بها فيحرم بغيرها كحجر

shave one part of a child's head and leave the remaining part unshaven."[60]

عَنْ عُمَرَ بْنِ نَافِعٍ، عَنْ نَافِعٍ، عَنِ ابْنِ عُمَرَ قَالَ: نَهَى رَسُولُ اللَّهِ صَلَّى اللهُ عَلَيْهِ وَ سَلَّمَ عَنِ الْقَزَعِ . قَالَ: وَمَا الْقَزَعُ؟ قَالَ: أَنْ يُحْلَقَ مِنْ رَأْسِ الصَّبِيِّ مَكَانٌ وَيُتْرَكَ مَكَانٌ

b. *Imitation of non-Muslims* (*tashabbuh* / تشبه): this is impermissible (e.g. imitating cults, religious groups, religious figures like Hindu pundits, Buddhist monks, etc.). This is based on the hadith of the Prophet (saw): **"whoever imitates a people is from among them…"**[61]

عَنِ ابْنِ عُمَرَ، قَالَ: قَالَ رَسُولُ اللَّهِ صَلَّى اللهُ عَلَيْهِ وَ سَلَّمَ: مَنْ تَشَبَّهَ بِقَوْمٍ فَهُوَ مِنْهُمْ

c. *Unusual hairstyle* (*shuhra* / شهرة): this is impermissible due to its eccentricity, unusual style and oddness (e.g. multi-coloured hair or large gelled spikes, etc.) based on the *hadith* from Ibn 'Umar (ra) that the Prophet (saw) said: **"whoever wears clothes to show off, Allah will clothe him in the same manner on the Day of Judgment."**[62]

عَنِ ابْنِ عُمَرَ، - قَالَ فِي حَدِيثِ شَرِيكٍ: يَرْفَعُهُ - قَالَ: «مَنْ لَبِسَ ثَوْبَ شُهْرَةٍ أَلْبَسَهُ اللَّهُ يَوْمَ الْقِيَامَةِ ثَوْبًا مِثْلَهُ

- Therefore, if a haircut is not half-shaven, nor imitates non-Muslims and is not to show off or

---

[60] See the *Sunan* of Ibn Majah (#2948): Ibn 'Abidin states in *Radd al-Muhtar*, 6:407:

وَيُكْرَهُ الْقَزَعُ وَهُوَ أَنْ يَحْلِقَ الْبَعْضَ وَيَتْرُكَ الْبَعْضَ

[61] Abu Dawud, Sunan (#4031).
[62] Abu Dawud, Sunan (#4029-4030).

eccentric, *then in general*, the haircut will be permissible.

8. **Trousers above the ankles**: It is preferable to have the trousers above the ankles but to have it *ordinarily* over them without any notion of pride or arrogance which the *hadiths* of the Prophet mention, does not entail sin although it will be deemed mildly disliked (*makruh tanzihi*) or contrary to what is better (*khilaf al-awla*).[63]

9. **Studying fashion design**: It is permitted to study fashion design as long as no Shariah aspects are contravened such as modelling semi-clad persons or being in unlawful places.

10. **Football T-Shirts**: It is generally permitted to wear shirts of football clubs although those sponsored by businesses that are contrary to Shariah like alcohol (Carlsberg, Budweiser, etc.) should be avoided as it would be a form of advertisement/endorsement of something unlawful.

---

[63] See al-'Ayni, '*Umdat al-Qari Sharh Sahih al-Bukhari*, 21:297:

وهذا مطلق يجب حمله على المقيد وهو ما كان للخيلاء

See also Mawlana Khalil Ahmad Sahranpuri, *Badhal al-Majhud*, 16:411: "The scholars state that it is recommended to have the garment or robe hang as far as half way down the shin and beyond that up to the ankles is permitted without any dislike in it. As for if it hangs below the ankles, then this is not allowed. If it should be out of pride or arrogance, then this amounts to a prohibition and if not out pride or arrogance, then it is mildly disliked…"

قال العلماء المستحب في الإزار والثوب إلى نصف الساقين، والجائز بلا كراهة ما تحته إلى الكعبين، فما نزل عن الكعبين فهو ممنوع، فإن كان للخيلاء فهو ممنوع منع تحريم، وإلا فمنع تنزيه

11. **Branded clothing**: In general it is permitted to wear branded clothing (e.g. Nike, Adidas, Puma, etc.) unless the brand is: (i) specifically against Islam and Islamic interests; (ii) is openly linked with immorality and (iii) directly supports the enemies of Islam.

12. **Pig skin:** clothing made out of pig skin even after tanning is not permissible. Salah with such clothing on will not be valid either.

13. **Fur clothing**: it is generally permitted to wear fur clothing. Those made from cruel treatment of animals should be avoided.

14. **Counterfeit clothes**: It is not permitted to purchase stolen goods nor is it permitted to wear clothing that have been deliberately manufactured through fraud and counterfeit measures.

15. **Logos and clothes**: any clothes with logos such as the Ralph Lauren polo player, the puma animal, etc. are permitted to wear as the image is 'unclear' and 'indistinct' i.e. small enough for it to be excused because the limbs are not plainly visible to an onlooker. However, it would be better to avoid wearing them when offering the *salah*.

16. **Artificial silk**: it is permitted to wear artificial silk.

17. **Wearing Suede**: if the suede material is made from other than pig skin, it will be permitted.

18. **Lingerie clothing**: this is permitted for a woman to wear for her spouse.

§10. The Politics of Clothing:
The Veil Controversy

———— ♦ ————

- Muslim attire like many aspects of Islam – whether that is Shariah Law, Jihad, the Caliphate, the Prophet (saw) himself – has been a point of open attack and criticism by Western countries for nearly two decades with the UK being no exception.

- The UK 'veil controversy' of 2006 generated by Jack Straw MP[64] and the re-merged *l'affaire du voile islamique* in France leading to the eventual face veil ban in 2010 have highlighted the irresponsible manner in which governments raise and address Islamic issues.[65]

- The veil issue is, as with many issues related to Islam, embedded in a wider political context of attempting to alter and undermine Islamic precepts and values which is evident in both government statements and policy. It is also a way to deflect and obscure more troubling matters of both UK and Western foreign policy

---

[64] See for example:

1. "Remove Full Veil Urges Straw" at http://news.bbc.co.uk/1/hi/uk_politics/6058672.stm
2. "Blair's Concern over Face Veils" at http://news.bbc.co.uk/1/hi/uk_politics/6058672.stm

[65] For outlines on the Europe's controversy with the veil, refer to C. Joppke's study *Veil: Mirror of Identity*; J. W. Scott, *The Politics of the Veil*, pp.1-20; Integrating Islam: Political and Religious Challenges in Contemporary France, J. Laurence and J. Vaisse, pp.1-14 and *Islam and the Veil: Theoretical and Regional Contexts*, ed. by T. Gabriel and R. Hannan, pp.1-4.

effects as well as their motives for action in international affairs.[66]

- Below are at least three areas to consider in the veil controversy: (i) fallacious arguments against the veil; (ii) what to avoid in the controversy and (iii) the wider political context.

Fallacies: *very bad arguments*

Argument 1:

[P1] A woman wearing the veil (*niqab*) is counterproductive to society.

Therefore,
[C1] Wearing a veil should be banned.

Response:

- It is not altogether clear how wearing a face veil hinders progression of society. It also does not follow at all that a veil obstructs necessary social interactions like buying and selling, being employed or ordinary mundane interactions (e.g. shopping, attending class, picking up the kids, driving, etc.). There is no logical link between a veil and counter-productivity in as much as there is with sunglasses, a wig and dressing gowns. Therefore the argument's conclusion does not strictly follow from its premise.

---

[66] P. Morey and A. Yaqin, *Framing Muslims: Stereotyping and Representation After 9/11*, pp.1-17.

Argument 2:

[P2] I find a woman wearing the veil (*niqab*) to be unsettling and disturbing and it creates barriers to communication.

―――――――――――――

Therefore,
[C2] Wearing a veil should be banned.

Response:

- It is not altogether clear how wearing a face veil hinders communication in as much as a phone call or radio does. It does not follow at all that a veil obstructs required social communications, i.e. 'I must see a face to be able to talk to it'. This kind of argument is a species of a 'mind-projection fallacy' or 'psychologist's fallacy' in that a person's own personal and situational fears as well as prejudices (whether historical or engendered) are translated as being objective features of reality or the way things are. Therefore, the fault does not lie in the veil but those who have misconceptions and fears about it.

Argument 3:

[P2] I find a woman wearing the veil (*niqab*) contradictory to my British/Western values.

―――――――――――――

Therefore,
[C2] Wearing a veil should be banned.

Response:

- How one feels and whether that is right is a matter of debate. Mere feelings are not an intellectually strong basis for grounding moral truths (cf. the 'Boo! – Hurrah!' theory of ethics). Also, the British/Western values are not the objective yardstick of measuring what is right and wrong and like any other value-system is not immune from critique. Moreover, it is also not altogether clear how the face veil even contradicts 'British/Western values'; that statement itself is not clear. Finally, drafting legislation based on outrage and emotions is equally weak and dangerous.

Argument 4:

[P2] I find a woman wearing the veil (*niqab*) a symbol of repression and subjugation.

Therefore,
[C2] Wearing a veil should be banned.

Response:

- An individual's personal feelings about the veil do not make an argument true. It is not accurate to make an unwarranted assumption about a class of people merely from reference to their clothing. By asking those who wear it will easily lift the misconception regarding it being worn. Moreover, there is no intrinsic connection between the woman's face veil and female subjugation; the link is *forged* through cultural images and a typified discourse on women by Western intellectuals. Many Muslim women wear the face veil out of a deep sense of religious observance and submission to Allah. Thus banning the veil out of a false and manufactured perception of associating it with subjugation is both far-fetched and incredulous. It most certainly is not intellectual. What is also hidden in the argument is that not making oneself sexually attractive is somehow repressive, unnatural and offensive. But why should that be the case? That is only a cultural understanding; it is not universal in any way.

Red-herrings and distractions: *what to avoid*

1. *Discussing the legal evidences surrounding the face veil*: i.e. the strength of the legal deductions from jurists that consider it as a mandatory (*wajib*) item of clothing.

    ——— this detracts from the context of the attack on Muslim dress and directs focus inwards into dogmatic discussions and unnecessary creation of sectarian tendencies within Muslim circles. This is also counterproductive for unifying against injustice and propaganda against Islam.

2. *Thinking the veil is a cultural item of clothing from Arabia*: i.e. it is a pre-Islamic Arabian custom that carried into Islamic practice and so has no primacy for being appropriated into part of normative Muslim dress.

    ——— the veil was part of the clothing of the best of women, the Mothers of the Believers, the Pure Wives of our Prophet (saw). Moreover, the veil is an item of clothing legislated by Allah and established from the Islamic sources and is not a mere adoption of Arab cultural norms of dress.

3. *Endorsing a 'varied Islam' idea*: i.e. that there is no normative body of law (i.e. rulings that transcend cultural proclivities) but that all Shariah laws are based on different interpretations of scriptural references by scholars that suit the context and climate of their time. Clothing and dress is no different; if we can articulate interpretations that accord with a 'modesty' in clothing that is congruent with the British/Western context then this would be equally valid and ideal; equally Islamic.

―――― where there is legitimate difference and legal diversity within the Islamic tradition, this should be upheld but to argue that there are no normative laws in Islam pertaining to clothing and dress is to oppose the Islamic consensus and tradition. Moreover supporting an indigenous version of Islam, depoliticised, secular and disconnected from a global struggle for restoration of Islamic political fortunes is to take the route of failure and degeneration.

4. *Discarding the veil*: i.e. openly urging Muslims to discard the veil and show openness and transparency in order to allay public fears and difficulties.

―――― this attitude is tantamount to irreverence against Allah's injunctions. The veil is not baseless and so a believer ought to defend the Islamic veil as an

Islamic opinion – even if it is not his own – and not to attack or malign it.[67]

Context: *The Problematic Muslim Subject*

- 'Muslim visibility': Muslims are a problematic presence in UK/Western societies with a growing trend of Muslims reverting back to Islamic beliefs, standards and principles and articulating their way of life as an alternative to that of their host nation. This is argued by the government and government funded think tanks as the precursor to 'radicalisation' or 'terrorism' (cf. the conveyor belt fallacy: 'the more Islamic you become, the more of a threat you become to national security').

- 'Muslim dissidence': Muslims trouble Western values like liberalism, individual freedom and rights because they are neither convinced of it intellectually nor adopt it as part of their own value-system seeing the contradiction and inherent flaws in them. This dissent is considered as being antithetical to community cohesion and integration as well as a threat to UK-British values. Therefore the only way to get Muslims to accept is to bully them into submitting to UK/Western values or force a change in legislation to specifically target the coomunity.

---

[67] As in the case of the shaykh al-Azhar Sayyid Tantawi who openly opposed the face veil and called for its removal in Islamic seminaries. He also upheld France's ban on the headscarf in schools. See for example "Egyptians Voices: 'Niqab veil Ban'" at http://news.bbc.co.uk/1/hi/world/middle_east/8291437.stm and "Was Egypt's Sheikh Tantawi a Liberal or a Stooge" at http://news.bbc.co.uk/1/hi/world/middle_east/8560149.stm.

- 'Reductive tropes': Muslims are framed in abstract stereotypes that endorse and perpetuate myths and historical prejudices borrowed from historical settings of the Crusades and the West's first bemused and hostile encounter with Islam made more poignant post-9/11 and 7/7; Muslims are seen therefore as: foreign, barbaric, fanatical, radical, queer, oppressed, duplicitous terrorists and threatening, etc.[68]

- 'Engage but rebuke' tactic: where MPs, politicians, Think Tanks, cultural commentators and key media figures make reckless and inappropriate comments about Islam to 'engage' and 'create debate' but frame the debate through contorted channels that make a reciprocal flow of discussion meaningless. Also, any dissenting Islamic voice is censured and censored creating a chronic one-sided debate.

- 'Attack Islam to change Islam': where key markers of Islam or Islamic symbols are maligned and criticised in order to prompt Muslims to re-evaluate their normativity (cf. Jihad as 'violent'; Caliphate system as 'medieval' or Shariah as 'barbaric').

Thus, although the veil is seen as an easy target by many in that it is a visible symbol of Islam, what it in fact underscores is the fragility of liberal ideas and values and its failure to find fertile lodging within the Muslim community. The way governments approach, therefore, the 'Islamic question' is often to problematize discourse surrounding it or to bully Muslims into submission to liberalism. Both approaches have seriously failed.

---

[68] C. Allen, *Islamophobia*, pp.3-50.

[End].

Peace and Blessing upon our Master,
Allah's Mercy to the worlds,
Our Beloved Prophet Muhammad,
His Companions and Family
And all who follow them.

S. Z. Chowdhury,
London 2010.

KEY REFERENCES

Arabic References:

Ibn 'Abidin, *Hashiyat Radd al-Muhtar 'ala 'l-Durr al-Mukhtar Sharh Tanwir al-Absar*, 7 vols. Beirut: Dar al-Ihya' al-Turath al-'Arabi, n.d.

——— *Radd al-Muhtar 'ala 'l-Durr al-Mukhtar*, 8 vols. Karachi: H. M. S. Co., 1986.

al-'Asqalani, *Fath al-Bari Sharh Sahih al-Bukhari* (Baz and 'Abd al-Baqi edn.), 15 vols. Beirut: Dar al-Kutub al-'Ilmiyya, 1997.

al-Haythami, *Majma' al-Zawa'id*, Cairo: Maktbat al-Qudsi, n.d.

——— al-Haythami, *Majma' al-Zawa'id*, Beirut: Dar al-Kitab al-'Arabi, 1982.

Ibn al-Humam, *Fath al-Qadir li 'l-'Ajiz al-Faqir Sharh al-Hidaya*, 9 vols. Beirut: Dar al-Ihya' al-Turath al-'Arabi, 1997.

al-Kasani, *al-Bada'i' al-Sana'i' fi Tartib al-Shara'i'*, 6 vols. Beirut: Dar al-Ihya' al-Turath al-'Arabi, 2000.

al-Marghinani, *al-Hidaya Sharh Bidyat al-Mubtadi*, 4 vols. Beirut: Dar al-Kutub al-'Ilmiyya, 2000.

Mawlana Nizam, et al. *al-Fatawa al-Hindiyya*, 6 vols. Quetta: Maktaba Majdiyya, 1983.

——— *al-Fatawa al-Hindiyya*, repr. Beirut: Dar al-Fikr, 1979.

——————— *al-Fatawa al-Hindiyya*, 6 vols. Beirut: Dar Ihya' Turath al-'Arabi, 1980.

al-Mawsili, *Kitab al-Ikhtiyar li-Ta'lil al-Mukhtar*, 5 vols. Cairo: Dar al-Ma'rifa, 2000.

al-Maydani, *al-Lubab fi Sharh al-Kitab*, 4 vols. Karachi: Kutub Khana, n.d.

al-Nawawi, *Sharh Sahih Muslim*, 18 vols. Beirut: Dar Ihya' al-Turath al-'Arabi, 1972.

Ibn Nujaym, *al-Bahr al-Ra'iq fi Sharh Kanz al-Daqa'iq*, 9 vols. Beirut: Dar al-Kutub al-'Ilmiyya, 1997.

al-Qal'aji, M. et al, *Mu'jam al-Lughat al-Fuqaha'*, Beirut: Dar al-Nafa'is, 2000.

al-Quduri, *al-Mukhtasar* (English-Arabic text, trans. M. Kiani, London: Dar al-Taqwa, 2009).

al-Shurunbulali, *Nur al-Idah* (English-Arabic text, trans. W. Charkawi) n.p. 2004.

——————— *Maraqi al-Falah Sharh Nur al-Idah*, Damascus: Maktabat al-'Ilm al-Hadith, 2001.

——————— *Maraqi al-Falah Sharh Nur al-Idah*, Beirut: Dar al-Kutub al-'Ilmiyya, 1995.

——————— *Imdad al-Fattah Sharh Nur al-Idah*, Damascus, n.p. 2001.

——————— *Maraqi al-Sa'adat*, Beirut: Dar al-Kutub al-Lubnani, 1973 and English trans. by F. A. Khan, London: Whitethread Press, 2010.

———— *Sabil al-Falah fi Sharh Nur al-Idah*, Beirut: Dar al-Bayruti, n.d.

Usmani, M. T. *Takmilat Fath al-Mulhim*, 3 vols. Karachi: Maktabat-i Dar al-'Ulum, 1986-1987.

Urdu References:

Farid, Muhammad. *Fatawa Faridiyya*, 5 vols. Pakistan: Dar al-'Ulum Publications, 2004-2009.

Gangohi, Mahmud Hasan, *Fatawa Mahmudiyya*, 25 vols. Karachi: Dar al-Ifta' Jamia Faruqiyya, n.d.

Jalalpuri, Sa'id Ahmad. *Fatawa Khatme Nabuwwat*, 3 vols. Multan: Alim-e Majlis Khatme Nabuwwat, 2005.

Khan, Ahmed Reza. *al-'Ataya li-Nabawiyya fi' l-Fatawa al-Ridwiyya*, 6 vols. Mubarakpur: Sunni Darul Isha'at, 1981.

———— *al-'Ataya al-Nabawiyya fi' l-Fatawa al-Ridwiyya*, 12 vols. Faisalabad: Maktaba Nuriyya Ridwiyya.

Kifayatullah, Muhammad. *Kifayat al-Mufti*, 10 vols. Karachi: Dar al-Isha'at, 2001.

Lajpuri, Abd al-Rahim. *Fatawa Rahimiyya*, 10 vols. Karachi: Darul Isha'at, 2009.

Ludhianvi, Rashid Ahmad. *Ahsan al-Fatawa*, Karachi: H. M. S. Co, 1398–.

Ludhianvi, Muhammad Yusuf. *Apke Masa'il Aur Unka Hal*, 10 vols. Karachi: Maktabat al-Ludhianwi, 1995-2002.

Qasmi, Mujahid al-Islam. *Fatawa Qadi*, Delhi: IFA Publications, 2004.

Sahranpuri, Khalil Ahmad. *Fatawa Mazahir 'Ulum* (= *Fatawa Khaliliyya*), Karachi: Maktabat Shaykh, n.d.

Usmani, Zafar Ahmad. *Imdad al-Ahkam*, 4 vols. Sahranpur: Deoband Publications, 1991.

Bengali References:

Mansur al-Haqq, *Fatawa Rahmaniyya*, 2 vols. Dhaka: Maktabat al-Ashraf-Rahmaniyya Publications, 1428 AH.

Mahmud al-Hasan, ed. *Bishoy Bhittik Mas'ala*, Dhaka: Mina Book House, 2000.

NOTES

Printed in Great Britain
by Amazon.co.uk, Ltd.,
Marston Gate.